Safeguarding
Learning & development

Framework 2021

THE CHURCH
OF ENGLAND

HOUSE OF BISHOPS

Published 23 April 2021

Next review 2024

Contents

Preface

Dear Colleagues,

I have great pleasure in introducing our new Safeguarding Learning and Development Framework, which was approved by the National Safeguarding Steering Group on 22 April 2021.

Effective safeguarding learning is one of the key means by which we will become a safer and healthier Church. It can be truly transformational and the learning pathways in our Framework aim to achieve this.

This Framework is the result of the creativity and hard work of a wide range of colleagues from across the Church. A great many people from all parts of the Church have contributed their time, ideas and passion to the development of this Framework. We are very grateful to everyone concerned, especially as they were helping to introduce change at a time of significant challenge with the Church facing the Covid pandemic.

Thank you very much for your help and feedback during the development phase, and for your support now in delivering the new Framework. Please remember that the Safeguarding Learning and Development Managers in the National Safeguarding Team are always available to assist you with the implementation of this Framework, as we continue our journey together to become a safer Church.

With my thanks for all you are doing and my prayers and best wishes,

The Rt Revd Dr J R Gibbs

Lead Bishop for Safeguarding

Introduction

This Framework sets out details of the Church's safeguarding learning pathways, and expectations of Church officers[1] in respect of those pathways.

The Church has an ambition to make a paradigm shift in its relationship with safeguarding. This requires recognition that safeguarding needs to move away from something that is in some respects external/imposed upon the Church, to something that flows from within the soul of the Church. Safeguarding is at the centre of our faith, in our practice, in our worship, in our praying, and in our believing. In other words, safeguarding needs to become integral to the very DNA of the Church rather than an appendage, with good safeguarding behaviours flowing naturally and intuitively. Theology, by which we simply mean clear thinking about God and the faith we share, has been interwoven into all our learning and the development pathways. As the Independent Inquiry into Child Sexual Abuse (IICSA) identified, this will require a significant shift in the Church's culture.

Achieving a paradigm shift in safeguarding requires a "whole system" approach within which change is achieved by the inter-relatedness of different strands. One developmental strand is "safeguarding learning". This framework sets out the form that safeguarding learning needs to take to contribute effectively to the paradigm shift envisioned and to overall organisational change. The safeguarding learning pathways support participants in developing and maintaining the necessary values, beliefs, knowledge, and skills to safeguard and protect children, young people, and vulnerable adults[2] as outlined in the 'Promoting a Safer Church' House of Bishops policy statement (2017).

It replaces and updates the 'House of Bishops Learning and Development Framework Practice Guidance' (2015) and the second and third editions of this document published in January 2017 and July 2019. The revisions to this edition are driven by a programme of change designed to strengthen the opportunities for learning and development in safeguarding.

The Framework sets out:

- The vision, model, standards and requirements for safeguarding learning and development in the Church context.

- Details of the range of learning and development pathways available and the requirements for their delivery.

- Details of additional learning and development opportunities.

This practice guidance is for use across all Church bodies[3].

Once published in 2021, Church bodies must plan for full implementation of this framework from January 2022. The framework will not be revised again until 2024, ready for the next three-yearly cycle of safeguarding learning to commence in 2025.

---

[1]   A 'Church officer' is anyone appointed/elected by or on behalf of the Church to a post or role, whether they are ordained or lay, paid or unpaid.

[2]   In their policies and procedures our statutory partners have now moved away from the terminology of 'vulnerable adults' towards 'adults at risk of harm', usually shortened to 'adults at risk'.

[3]   'Church bodies' includes parishes, dioceses, cathedrals, religious communities, theological education institutions, National Church Institutions (NCIs) and other associated bodies.

What is the Status and Structure of this Document?

This document is safeguarding guidance issued by the House of Bishops under section 5 of the Safeguarding and Clergy Discipline Measure 2016. It is intended that section 5 will be amended in 2021[4], but as the law currently stands all relevant persons must have due regard to guidance issued by the House of Bishops on matters relating to the safeguarding of children and vulnerable adults.

Relevant persons[5] are:

- A clerk in Holy Orders who is authorised to officiate in accordance with the Canons of the Church of England.

- A diocesan, suffragan, or assistant bishop.

- An archdeacon.

- A person who is licensed to exercise the office of reader or serve as a lay worker.

- A churchwarden.

- A parochial church council.

A duty to have "due regard" to guidance means that the person under the duty is not free to disregard it but is required to follow it unless there are cogent reasons for not doing so. "Cogent" for this purpose means clear, logical, and convincing.

Failure to have "due regard" to House of Bishops' safeguarding guidance may be considered misconduct under the Clergy Discipline Measure 2003 (CDM), may be grounds for the revocation of a reader's or lay worker's licence by the Bishop, or may result in an investigation being carried out by the Charity Commission, and the churchwarden or PCC members may be subject to disqualification as charity trustees.

This document is written for those responsible for implementing, or co-ordinating the implementation of, the guidance issued by the House of Bishops but especially for those providing, or co-ordinating the provision of, training on safeguarding matters.

---

[4] It is intended to amend the law to allow the House of Bishops to put in place a new code of practice on safeguarding children and vulnerable adults which will specify both requirements (which will be mandatory) and guidance (which will be advisory). The amendments will also expand the categories of person to whom the section applies.

[5] Cathedral chapters will be added to this list when the draft Cathedrals Measure comes into force, which we expect to happen in 2021.

1 Our Vision for Safeguarding Learning

1.1 Transformative learning

Learning should be transformative and impactful but, in many sectors (local authority, police, health), has historically had a strong focus on the explanation of facts and processes. Organisational safeguarding failures have historically been responded to by national government and local statutory bodies by the creation of new processes and procedures – "training" is then delivered to explain them. These organisations are often then surprised when, despite high levels of training, the same quality of practice continues. In other words, the training has not led to a change in behaviour.

Over the last five years in secular practice, there has been a major shift in the approach to training. There has been a realisation that learning opportunities should focus on people's beliefs and values and not just ensure that processes are understood. People's behaviours flow from their beliefs and values – if the aim is to achieve "good" safeguarding behaviours, it is necessary to engage people at this deeper level. This is called "second order" change; this happens when people do things not because they will get into trouble if they do not, but because there is an inner drive and motivation to behave in a particular way.

People should leave a learning experience in some way different from the way they entered. The safeguarding learning and development pathways for the Church have been developed with this intention.

In terms of methodology, this principle will mean a greater focus on:

- "Self-reflexivity" – whereby participants spend time in personal reflection on a safeguarding issue, connecting it to their beliefs, values and their own life experiences and characteristics which shape them and how they make sense of the world; then working this through to the implications for their behaviours.

- "Dialogue" – whereby the participants are facilitated to engage in a depth of sharing of experience and perspectives through which they create wisdom and meaning.

- The voice(s) of victims and of survivors – see below.

- The theological underpinnings of good safeguarding behaviours.

1.2 Survivors have a key role to play in the development and delivery of transformative learning

The impact of survivor and victim involvement – as "experts by experience" – is transformative and significant in contributing to the second order change detailed above. It is also fundamental to the development of healthy and safe cultures within Church communities that the voices of victims and survivors are heard and considered at every step of our learning and development journey. Best practice would be for safeguarding learning to be co-designed and co-delivered with survivors.

1.3 Learning is a journey with an outcome, not an event

As part of the development and revision of the learning and development framework we consider safeguarding learning to have four elements:

- Preparation: what participants need to do at the outset of the learning journey so that they maximise the gain they get from direct inputs.
- Learning: the methodologies and techniques used to achieve learning outcomes.
- Application: embedding the learning: how participants are supported to apply the learning.
- Evaluation: evidencing that the learning is making a difference to beliefs and behaviours.

1.4 Safeguarding trainers are crucial

The impact of safeguarding learning will, to a large extent, be determined by the investment of Church bodies in their local resource by ensuring they have the people with the right level of skills, experience and expertise to deliver transformative learning experiences. Those with learning responsibilities need to be properly supported, developed, and supervised.

1.5 Promoting positive cultures: a message from the Independent Inquiry into Child Sexual Abuse (IICSA)

Promoting healthy Christian cultures in all Church bodies needs to be an essential aim of our safeguarding learning. The 2020 IICSA Investigation Report[6] and other research evidence highlights the importance of organisational culture in getting safeguarding right. The kinds of unhealthy cultural attributes identified by IICSA (e.g., tribalism, clericalism, deference, naivety, focus on reputation, fear, and secrecy about sexuality) were part of our Church culture's DNA. These unhealthy attributes identified by IICSA increase the likelihood of abuse taking place, are barriers to positive prevention of abuse and perpetuate poor responses to victims and survivors. Healthy organisational cultural attributes, on the other hand, are a protective shield against those who would abuse or cover up abuse. They promote the proactive and loving behaviours which prevent abuse and help survivors to heal.

Promoting healthy Christian cultures will therefore be a golden thread running through all safeguarding pathways.

---

6   The Anglican Church Investigation Report | IICSA Independent Inquiry into Child Sexual Abuse

2   Safeguarding Learning

2.1   Elements of safeguarding learning

Core safeguarding learning pathways (Basic Awareness, Foundation, Leadership and Senior Leadership) have been developed as a modular programme which builds learning according to role. Therefore, these pathways should be completed in consecutive order until an individual has reached the required highest level of learning for their role.

Additional safeguarding learning pathways have been developed to further enhance safeguarding knowledge in specific practice areas, or for specific roles.

For consistency of delivery and content, safeguarding learning pathways will be produced and released for implementation by the National Safeguarding Team (NST) by way of "training for trainers" sessions. Church bodies will be asked to identify "trainers for training" by the NST. Safeguarding learning support visits will be offered to Church bodies at regular intervals by the National Safeguarding Learning and Development Managers.

It is expected that people work to achieve the required level of learning as soon as is practicable upon starting a new role. For example, PCC members often end up standing for election on the day and their appointment takes effect immediately. It is not therefore realistic to say that they must be trained before they start. The required core safeguarding learning pathways should be a priority with Basic Awareness and Foundation being completed as part of an induction process and the remaining core pathways being completed within six months of an individual taking up a post.

Refresher learning should be completed at a three-yearly interval and will keep knowledge and skills up to date. It is expected that everyone will have been trained to the required level within each three-yearly cycle. Refresher learning should be undertaken at the highest required level (as per safeguarding training in the statutory sector) for core pathways. Additional pathways should also be refreshed on a three-yearly cycle. National learning pathways will be updated as required by changes in practice and to supplement the programme of learning.

2.2 National Safeguarding Training Portal[7]

The Safeguarding Training Portal hosts the core Basic Awareness and Foundation online learning pathways, and the additional Safer Recruitment and People Management and Raising Awareness of Domestic Abuse pathways.

During 2021 the portal is being developed to provide a basic learning management function for Church bodies to co-ordinate their delivery of the Leadership Pathway. The portal's reporting function enables those with the required level of permission to run reports detailing completions of each course for their Church body.

The portal also contains the in-person pathway materials for download and use for local delivery. The additional resources area of the portal includes a virtual library of resources, signposting to other safeguarding related learning opportunities (e.g. The Clewer Initiative materials on modern-day slavery), useful websites and helplines for further information and support.

2.3 Planning

Each Church body should develop a three-year Safeguarding Learning and Development Strategy to capture the numbers of people requiring each learning pathway which will in turn inform the number of learning opportunities and level of resources required to meet the assessed levels of need.

The questions below could be used to inform your learning strategy and structure your analysis.

1   In addition to the Church's learning pathways, are there local needs we need to plan for?

2   Which roles require which pathway/s?

3   How many people do we have in each role?

4   When did those people last receive training?

5   How many times do we need to run the pathway each year to meet the assessed level of need?

6   What is our local resource/capacity? Have we got the right skills and volume – including direct delivery, administrative support, equipment, IT systems etc?

7   How do we secure additional resources if needed?

8   Our plans to develop a pool of experienced and skilled volunteer facilitators.

---

[7]   The National Safeguarding Training Portal is found at https://safeguardingtraining.cofeportal.org

9   How are we going to involve survivors and relevant organisations (e.g. domestic abuse organisations) in the delivery of learning pathways?

10   How does this strategy relate to the safeguarding learning strategies of other local Church bodies and of multi-agency safeguarding partnerships?

To ensure that safeguarding is embedded across the Church, the Safeguarding Learning and Development Strategy, and how it is delivered, should be developed in conjunction with the broader training strategies of other relevant Church bodies. For ordinands and trainee readers, all safeguarding pathways should be integrated into Initial Ministerial Education (IME) phases 1 and 2, and this will require partnership between TEIs and dioceses. As an example, a prospective ordinand would be expected to complete the Basic Awareness and Foundation pathways during discernment, prior to any placement and certainly before the Bishops' Advisory Panel. The Leadership Safeguarding Pathway should then be completed prior to ordination. They would then repeat the Leadership Pathway at three-yearly intervals and participate in additional safeguarding pathways as appropriate.

2.4   Delivery

Numbers and ratio of participants and facilitators for safeguarding pathways.

- There is a direct correlation between the ratio of facilitators/trainers to participants, the depth of engagement and quality of dialogue that can be achieved, and the consequent impact of the pathway.

- In traditional classroom training, where the trainer talks to a group with the aid of many PowerPoint slides, the ratio is less of an issue as participants are not being engaged in a dialogical or self-reflexive mode – rather, they are on the whole passive recipients of information. Such training can be useful e.g. to explain a process and to impart a set of facts. However, it is not "transformative"; it will not deliver cultural and behavioural change.

- The principles of this learning model do require depth of engagement and dialogue, as well as a trusting space, so ratios matter. The main reason is that this is intended to be **transformative** learning. In other words, it is intended to affect people's beliefs, values, and behaviours (rather than just imparting knowledge) and that requires a deeper level of engagement, reflection, trust, and dialogue than can be achieved with traditional "classroom/PowerPoint" approaches with larger numbers.

- With transformational learning the trainer's task is different compared with previous training: the primary focus is on **facilitating** dialogue and reflection so that the participants together develop safeguarding wisdom and meaning – rather than just **delivering** information. This means that to enable the trainer to be completely tuned in to each participant and how they are receiving and responding to the material, and then be able to support their engagement, smaller numbers are necessary. The safety dimension is also extremely important; responding well to people who are triggered/become distressed in a virtually delivered learning session is vital – too many people and even with two facilitators it will be difficult to respond well.

- The basic building blocks are:

  - that safeguarding pathways are delivered (virtually and in person) on a 1:6 ratio i.e. one facilitator working with up to six participants.

  - that any session with more than six people must have two facilitators.

- Each pathway then has an optimum number of people who can attend. For example, in the Leadership Pathway, when delivered virtually the optimum is 12. This means there needs to be two facilitators.

- To maximise available facilitation capacity, Church bodies can book more than the optimum attendance levels. If the target attendance level is 12, 16 participants can be booked. It is recognised that this means that on occasions the 1:6 ratio and optimum number attending will be slightly exceeded.

- With pathways that are delivered in-person, the intention is that group sizes can increase from 12 to 24. The facilitators will still work with participants in groups of 1:6 but because participants and facilitators are physically in the same space it should be possible for one facilitator to monitor and engage with two groups of six. As soon as in-person delivery is possible this will be trialled to identify the impact.

Summary of ratio and number of facilitators requirements

Optimum number of participants in the group	Optimum ratio of facilitator to participant	Maximum number that can be booked	Number of facilitators required
12 for virtual delivery	1:6 (Each facilitator working with one group of up to six)	16	2 (if more than six people participating)
24 for in-person delivery *To be trialled when in-person delivery is possible.* *It is accepted that there will be occasions when these numbers are exceeded if a high number of those booked turn up*	1:6 (Each facilitator working with two groups of up to six.) *To be trialled when in-person delivery is possible* *It is accepted that there will be occasions when these ratios are exceeded if a high number of those booked turn up*	28	2 (if more than six people participating)

Who delivers

Safeguarding learning must be facilitated by experienced and skilled people who understand safeguarding in respect of children and adults in a Church context **and** have the requisite training and facilitation expertise. No matter how good the actual pathway, it is the skills of the person facilitating delivery that will determine the actual learning impact achieved.

Diocesan/Cathedral Safeguarding Advisers must only lead on delivering training if they have the requisite skills to do so. If they cannot deliver training directly, they must ensure that they provide or co-ordinate the provision of training on safeguarding matters, as per their regulated responsibilities.[8] Many dioceses and cathedrals now have dedicated professional safeguarding trainers as part of their safeguarding team; this does represent best practice.

Capacity

Facilitation capacity can be increased through the development of a pool of skilled volunteers. Several dioceses have already done this and have found that their capacity for delivering has increased significantly as a result. For example, in St Edmundsbury and Ipswich, volunteers have been recruited in each deanery to lead the delivery of safeguarding learning in their specific locality. In Chichester, volunteers are commissioned by the Bishop as a way of marking the significant impact they have in extending the diocese's resources for training.

Ongoing oversight and support should be offered to volunteers to ensure that they are resourced for the important work they are undertaking and that learning standards are maintained. Oversight and support should include observations of delivery. In Sheffield, the Diocesan Safeguarding Trainer has a programme of training and ongoing support and supervision in place for their volunteers which is very well established.

In the different Church bodies consideration should be given to the best model to deliver the learning pathways. In some contexts, learning could be delivered across parishes or deaneries utilising volunteers and officially commissioning them where appropriate. Cathedrals and TEIs should consider, together with the dioceses, the best methods for ensuring that all relevant Church officers are engaged in the appropriate level of safeguarding learning, either by delivering independently or by sharing resources. Arrangements between Church bodies should be agreed and monitored by those involved to ensure that they are meeting identified needs.

Needs of participants in learning pathways

Those delivering safeguarding learning need to recognise that some participants will have needs which need to be understood and responded to appropriately and creatively.

---

8   See section 4 paragraph 1a-o of the Diocesan Safeguarding Advisors Regulations 2016.

Needs of Participants	Possible response
Participants may have experienced abuse or trauma themselves and be at risk of the learning pathway triggering them	Ensure that participants are aware that they are engaging in safeguarding learning and therefore there is a possibility that those who are victims/survivors may be triggered. Ensure that there is opportunity for participants to raise issues with facilitators before, during or after sessions. At the start of virtual sessions explain that it is possible for participants to turn off their video, mute themselves or withdraw if they need to. Ensure that any group of more than six people (for both virtual or in-person delivery) is facilitated by two-people. Offer an alternative way to access the learning, e.g. 1:1, rather than in a group context.
Visual or hearing impairments	Where training is completed online, the format of the material is such that all written content is also available audibly at the click of a button. Transcripts of audio files are also available. Large print versions of materials can be produced. For the pre-work elements of the learning pathways, it is possible for participants to record their responses in audio format and submit them in this way. They could also have a supporter who records their responses for them. In-person training of more than six participants must be delivered by two people as explained in section 2.4 in order that appropriate support can be offered. Participants may also wish to bring along a supporter or require a signer who can assist them during the training to engage in the materials. This should be arranged in advance of attendance at safeguarding training. Lack of access to computers or other equipment
Lack of access to computers or other equipment	The Basic Awareness and Foundation pathways are available in both online and in-person training formats. Arrange for participants to attend an agreed office or location to access computer equipment. It is also possible for participants to complete pre-work in audio format, by hand and submit them by post. Learning sessions could be completed on a one-to-one basis via telephone.
Literacy or other learning needs	For the pre-work elements of the learning pathways, it is possible for participants to record their responses in audio format and submit them in this way. If available to them, participants could use dictation software to enable them to say their responses to questions and have software write this for them – this functionality is available using the "dictate" function in Microsoft Word for example. They could also have a supporter who records their responses for them. In-person training of more than six participants must be delivered by two people as explained in section 2.4 in order that appropriate support can be offered. Participants may also wish to bring along a supporter who can assist them during the training to engage in the materials, this should be arranged in advance of attendance at safeguarding training. Trainers could produce material on different colour backgrounds or provide overlay laminates for people with dyslexia.
English is not a participant's first language	Materials could be translated into an alternative language. A supporter/translator could be provided either in-person or via telephone system. Consideration could be given to running sessions for those who speak specific languages, if appropriate or if demand warrants it.

2.5   Pathway fidelity and local flexibility of delivery

The expectation is that Church bodies will deliver safeguarding pathways in a way that retains fidelity to the core elements of the pathway. Each pathway will specify what constitutes fidelity to the core elements – please see the tables in sections 3 and 4.

Should a Church body implement the pathways without fidelity, they will no longer be pathways approved by the NST.

This is important because there needs to be consistency across the Church that people are having the same learning experience. Without this, the Church is not able to give account to the wider community, survivors, or other parts of the Church as to the quality and efficacy of its safeguarding learning. To say a certain number of Church officers have completed a particular pathway becomes meaningless if core elements are different between different Church bodies. The Church will have no way of delivering Church-wide quality assurance of its safeguarding learning as it would not be comparing like with like.

At a local level, lack of fidelity has other risks. For example, when a priest moves from one area to another, if the Safeguarding Leadership Pathway they have experienced in the diocese/cathedral they came from is different to that in the diocese/cathedral they are going to, then the receiving diocese/cathedral has no way of knowing what learning that person has and whether they have completed learning to the required standard.

Moreover, without these standards, there is a real danger that decisions on safeguarding learning will be based on current resource availability rather than what is needed to make change happen.

Core material will be provided for each pathway, and facilitators' notes and training-for-trainers materials will be included. These base materials can be supplemented with locally relevant resources, case studies, exercises, etc. to bring the learning to life for the participants on each pathway delivered.

Flexibility in delivery is permitted in several ways:

- To maximise resources and ensure consistency of practice. For example: dioceses, cathedrals or Theological Education Institutions may wish to consider joint appointments of safeguarding trainers or sharing resources.

- To make material specific for the needs, demands, culture and location of the participant group. For example, case studies within a pathway could be altered for a role specific group to ensure that the examples used are specific to the context in which attendees are working. Different communication methods can be used when, for example, some participants might struggle with written work.

- To schedule and deliver learning opportunities in the best way possible to achieve maximum engagement. For example, utilising virtual delivery methods, in-person learning sessions or a combination of the two.

Where such amendments are proposed, the National Safeguarding Learning and Development Managers must be consulted.

2.6   Evaluation

The history and experience of evaluation in "safeguarding training" across all sectors, not just the Church, is that it tends to focus on the immediate self-reported capturing of people's experience of the session itself. The limitation of this is that we do not know if it is having any impact – do people just "attend" the event, tick that box, and carry on as before?

The evaluation that really matters is whether the "learning experience" has affected someone's beliefs, values and understanding at a deep level so that there is a change in the person's behaviours – they now do things not because they must do something, but because they really want to exhibit those behaviours. This is "second order" change – when people do things because there is an inner motivation. The purpose of evaluation, then, is to try to find out if any difference in behaviours has indeed been achieved. The level of evaluation required varies dependent on the pathway. Evaluation will be undertaken using The Kirkpatrick Evaluation Model. This was created by Donald Kirkpatrick, Ph.D., to define the four levels of evaluation. The four levels of evaluation are:

Level 1 – the reaction of the participant and their thoughts about the learning experience.

Level 2 – the participant's resulting learning and increase in knowledge from the learning experience.

Level 3 – the participant's behavioural change and improvement after applying the learning and skills; and

Level 4 – the results or effects that the participant's performance has on the organisation.

2.7   Monitoring attendance, successful completion, and engagement

Attendance

Attendance at safeguarding learning and development pathways needs to be recorded consistently and accurately to ensure that all attendees have a learning record. These records will enable refresher cycles to be identified and will facilitate the monitoring and quality assurance of safeguarding learning and development.

For clergy, their record of learning will be included in their personal file ('Blue File') and transferred with them if they move between locations throughout their ministry. Safeguarding learning information will be included by the Bishop in the Clergy Current Status Letter (CCSL).[9] Paragraph 37 of the Personal Files Relating to Clergy Guidance, 2018 edition, states 'A record of a cleric's safeguarding training must be retained on the personal file, including the exact nature of the training, the date the training was received and who provided the training'. Details of attendance must be passed from the Safeguarding Team to the Bishop's office to ensure that clergy files can be kept up to date. The record must certify whether the training received is compliant with NST requirements for fidelity. For ordinands and readers in training, safeguarding learning completed should feature in the final reports issued by TEIs. Where it is not, dioceses and cathedrals should be requesting this information to ensure that learning records are complete.

Definition of "successful completion"

Each pathway will specify what constitutes "successful completion". The Basic Awareness and Foundation online pathways have a 'pass' mark which must be achieved; this is set at 75%. Throughout the materials there are several questions to check knowledge ahead of the final assessment. Each of the questions contributes to the overall pass score. A certificate is automatically generated for those who reach or surpass the pass mark. Those who do not achieve the required pass mark are issued a 'certificate of referral'[10] which indicates that they must have a conversation with the Diocesan Safeguarding Adviser/Cathedral Safeguarding Adviser (DSA/CSA). As a result of this conversation a participant may be asked to take the whole pathway again to repeat the learning and achieve the pass mark, or the DSA/CSA could request that an individual is given a further attempt at the final assessment.

For safeguarding Leadership and Senior Leadership, completion means that individuals have engaged in all preparation work, submitted work required, engaged with all sessions, and completed the evaluation stage evidencing impact on behaviours. All of this is required

---

9   For information about Clergy Blue Files and CCSL, see 'Personal Files Relating to Clergy' (2018).

10   Certificates of referral are issued in less than 1.5% of course completions. For example: from 1 October 2020 to 8 January 2021 there were 6247 completions of the Basic Awareness Pathway. 79 certificates of referral were issued.

before someone receives written confirmation of completion via the issue of certificates. The renewal date for these pathways is then three years from the certificate issue date.

Successful completion of the additional pathways is determined within the fidelity to the model for each. This is detailed in the tables in Section 4.

Engagement

Where participants do not engage or are deliberately difficult or disruptive the facilitators are responsible for ensuring this behaviour is not accepted. Anyone attending who fails to participate or engage should be spoken to privately by the facilitators to ascertain if there are specific reasons for this. Where there are justifiable reasons for a person not participating or engaging, the person should be offered support or guidance including signposting to appropriate agencies/people and be offered the opportunity to complete their learning later. For those who do not have justifiable reasons it will be necessary and appropriate to report their non-participation or disengagement to the appropriate person, such as their diocesan bishop (for clergy), parish priest (for parish officers), supervisor or manager (for employees/volunteers). Those who do not fully participate or engage in the safeguarding learning requirements should not be issued with a certificate of successful completion and should be requested to repeat the learning later.

ATTENDANCE AT SAFEGUARDING LEARNING AND

DEVELOPMENT PATHWAYS NEEDS TO BE

RECORDED CONSISTENTLY AND ACCURATELY

SAFEGUARDING
Learning and Development Framework

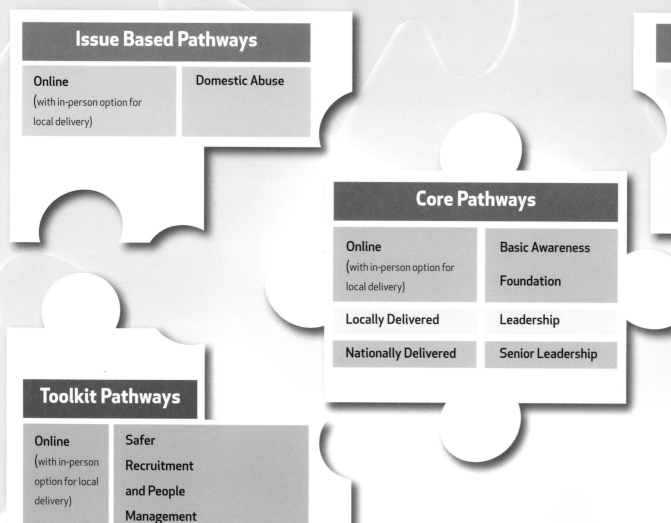

Issue Based Pathways

Online (with in-person option for local delivery)	Domestic Abuse

Role Specific Pathways

Locally Delivered	Permission to Officiate (inc. Readers with PtO)
	Parish Safeguarding Officer induction
Nationally Delivered	Link Person
	Support Person
	DDO/ADDO

Core Pathways

Online (with in-person option for local delivery)	Basic Awareness
	Foundation
Locally Delivered	Leadership
Nationally Delivered	Senior Leadership

Toolkit Pathways

Online (with in-person option for local delivery)	Safer Recruitment and People Management

Professional Development for Safeguarding Staff

Nationally Commisioned/ Delivered	DSA/CSA Development
	Trainers Development

3 Core Safeguarding Learning Pathways

The core learning pathways are a modular programme with the level of learning required being determined by the role and responsibilities of individuals. Those who hold positions of responsibility will require more in-depth learning than those who do not. For example, a member of clergy will require learning to Leadership level whereas a volunteer who is acting as an additional adult at a youth group session would require learning to Foundation level.

No accreditation is given against the core safeguarding learning pathways for prior learning, including in other denominations (except for the Methodist Church Foundation module). This is due to Church core safeguarding learning pathways situating safeguarding practice within the unique context of the Church of England and providing participants with the opportunity to relate their learning to their faith.

The Basic and Foundation pathways provide the essential learning necessary to recognise, respond, record, and refer safeguarding concerns. The Leadership and Senior Leadership pathways explore effective leadership behaviours and organisational culture issues in depth. However further learning may also be needed for some. Beyond the requirements of core safeguarding pathways, additional pathways – covering a range of subject areas – have been developed.

Basic Awareness and Foundation have both now been accredited by The CPD Certification Service. CPD stands for Continuing Professional Development CPD and is the term used to describe the learning activities professionals engage in to develop and enhance their abilities. It enables learning to become conscious and proactive, rather than passive and reactive.

The tables below set out, for each pathway, the following information:

- Pre-requisites for attendance at the pathway

- Delivery methods

- Learning outcomes

- Required attendees

- Recommended attendees

- Fidelity to the pathway

- Evaluation level

3.1 Basic Awareness

Pre-Requisites	Not Applicable
Delivery	**Online Pathway** (*Replica of online material available for in-person delivery in exceptional circumstances*)
Outcomes	• Connect the core principles and practices of safeguarding to the Christian faith. • Recognise issues of power and abuse as they present themselves in a range of contexts, including the Church. • Identify the barriers (emotional, psychological & theological) that can prevent the promotion of heathy Church communities. • Apply a clear process in the handling of concerns/safeguarding information whilst recognising the boundaries of their own role.
Required Attendees	• All Church Officers[11] • Anyone going on to complete any other safeguarding learning pathway.
Recommended Attendees	• Anyone wanting or needing a Basic Awareness of safeguarding.

Fidelity to the Pathway	**Online/Virtual Delivery**	**In-person Delivery**
	Completed online.	• In-person delivery in a single session by exception using the material provided by the NST. • Optimum group size of 24 with two facilitators.

Evaluation	Level 1 – Immediate feedback captured at the end of the learning pathway.

---

[11] A person appointed by the DBE as a Foundation Governor of a Church of England school is not required to undertake any diocesan safeguarding training in addition to the safeguarding training they are required to undertake as a school governor. A Foundation Governor must send a copy of their training completion certificate (or other evidence of their completion of the school governor safeguarding training) to the Diocesan Director of Education, or the DBE safeguarding lead, within [6] months of taking up their position as Foundation Governor and this must be retained by the DBE in its safeguarding training records.

However, where a person appointed by the DBE as a Foundation Governor of a Church of England school also holds another Church Officer role in the diocese or elsewhere in the national church they must, in addition to the training they may undertake as a school governor, also undertake any diocesan or other safeguarding training as may be required in relation to their other Church Officer role.

Pre-Requisites	Basic Awareness
Delivery	**Online Pathway** *(Replica of online material available for in-person delivery in exceptional circumstances)*
Outcomes	• Connect an understanding of good safeguarding practice to their own role and responsibilities. • Recognise commonalities and differences arising from the age or circumstances of those affected, and how this informs appropriate action. • Identify wider support, accountability, and governance arrangements relevant for safeguarding in their context. • Analyse and respond appropriately to a variety of safeguarding scenarios whilst recognising the boundaries of their own role.
Required Attendees	• Anyone holding the Bishop's licence, commission, authorisation, or permission (clergy, PtO, Readers, LLMs). • Anyone in a role which involves work with children, young people, or vulnerable adults. • Churchwardens. • Anyone going on to complete any other safeguarding learning pathway. • Pre-ordination or license students, prior to BAP or selection Panel. • Vergers. • PCC Members/Lay Chapter Members. • Staff at Theological Education Institutions with student facing roles. • Members of the Diocesan Safeguarding Advisory Panel.
Recommended Attendees	Not Applicable

Fidelity to the Pathway	**Online/Virtual Delivery**	**In-person Delivery**
	Completed online.	• In-person delivery in a single session by exception using the material provided by the NST. • Optimum group size of 24 with two facilitators.

Evaluation	Level 1 – Immediate feedback captured at the end of the learning pathway.

3.3   Leadership

Pre-Requisites	Basic Awareness and Foundation
Delivery	**Local delivery using a virtual platform or in-person learning sessions.**
Outcomes	<ul><li>Connect the Church's mission and theological foundations with what good leadership behaviour looks like in a safeguarding context.</li><li>Evaluate aspects of their own leadership practice and identify changes required which they then take forward with confidence.</li><li>Analyse what healthy Christian communities look like, how healthy communities keep people safe, and their role as leaders in shaping Christian communities that are healthy and safe.</li><li>Reflect on the impact that abuse and trauma have on individuals' lives, relationships, and interaction in a community setting.</li><li>Integrate their own faith, beliefs, and values with those underpinning good safeguarding behaviours.</li></ul>

Required Attendees

This is designed for those people who play a lead role in shaping the culture of the Church body concerned. This will always include:

- All clergy holding the Bishop's licence, commission, authorisation, or permission (including PtO where exemption has not been given) including Honorary/Assistant Bishops and Chaplains.
- All Readers and Licensed Lay Ministers holding the Bishop's licence (under Canons E6 & E8), together with all others who hold the Bishop's commission, authorisation, or permission to carry out similar ministerial functions (including PtO where exemption has not been given). (*Ordinands need to have completed the Leadership Pathway before their diaconal ordination and lay ministers in training before they are licensed.*)
- Non-executive members of Chapter (unless their role in the diocese requires a higher level).
- Safeguarding Officers/Leads in all Church bodies.
- Teaching staff at Theological Education Institutions who are delivering the Leadership Pathway.

It should also, according to the local context, include such other people who significantly influence the culture of that Church body. These may include, for example, lay ministry staff employed by a PCC or Bishops' Mission Order, locally appointed leaders of new worshipping communities, focal ministers, and Churchwardens*. The requirements for attendance for people in local leadership roles will be determined by agreement between the Bishop/Dean and their respective safeguarding adviser. Where there is a determination that someone must undertake this pathway, that person then becomes a required attendee.

* Whilst in many contexts the level of influence of Churchwardens may well not reach the threshold, it should be noted that this can increase significantly during vacancies.

At the point that in-person learning can resume, and the Senior Leadership Pathway is able to commence via in-person delivery, this pathway also becomes a pre-requisite for those to attend the Senior Leadership Pathway.

Recommended Attendees	Whilst in-person learning is not possible and senior leaders are completing a Virtual Safeguarding Senior Leadership Pathway the Leadership Pathway is recommended but not required for them.
Fidelity to the Pathway	**Online Virtual Delivery:** • Two 90-minute sessions delivered via Zoom, one-two weeks apart. • 2 facilitators. • Optimum number of participants: 12. • Pre-work completed and submitted before Session One. • Session One – the four questions are discussed as per the pathway. • Session Two – theological reflection is completed. Case study exercise is retained but a different case study could be used. Identifying three things learnt, three things to change. • Post Session Two – Watching documentary "Exposed – the Church's Darkest Secret" or completing some additional reading within four weeks. Evaluation (comprising personal reflection) completed 4-6 weeks after Session Two.	**In-person Delivery** A combination of both virtual and in-person delivery – • Pre-work completed and submitted before Session One. • Session One: 90-minute session, delivered virtually via Zoom by two facilitators to an optimum number of 12 participants. • Session One – the four questions are discussed as per the pathway. • Session Two – two-hour session to be delivered in-person by two facilitators to an optimum number of 24 participants. (Here the ratio of 1:6 can be maintained as participants and facilitators are physically in the same space. This means that small groups of 6 can be engaged with and monitored by the facilitators as they move between the groups, something which cannot be done effectively when delivery is virtual.) • Session Two – theological reflection is completed. Case study exercise is retained but a different case study could be used. • Post Session Two – Watching documentary "Exposed: The Church's Darkest Secret" or completing some additional reading within four weeks. Evaluation 4-6 weeks after Session Two is completed as set out in the pathway – to include 360 feedback.
Evaluation	Level 3 – Immediate feedback captured at the end of the learning pathway. Reflective evaluation tasks. Setting of safeguarding goals which can be discussed and reviewed by the DSA/CSA and during the person's developmental meetings over the next few years before their refresher is due **and/or** 360-degree feedback.

It is recognised that the exercise of PtO (for both retired clergy and readers) can vary considerably. For some it will involve a high level of work regularly, for others a very low level of work irregularly. As the main Safeguarding Leadership Pathway is now targeted at those people "who play a lead role in shaping the culture of the Church body concerned" those with PtO whose role meets this criterion must participate in the main Safeguarding Leadership Pathway. Those with PtO whose role does not meet this criterion must participate in a bespoke PtO Safeguarding Learning Pathway.

The decision about which Pathway someone with PtO should take must be made by the Bishop or Dean in consultation with the DSA/CSA and/or safeguarding trainer. The local supervisor (incumbent or rural dean) may also be well placed to assist in identifying the level of involvement of an individual and therefore which pathway would be most appropriate. For those newly retired, the Pathway individuals take should be decided at the point they start their new role. For existing PtOs a formal decision based on consideration of a person's role against the above criterion would need to be made within the diocese.

3.4   Senior Leadership

Pre-Requisites	Basic Awareness, Foundations, and Leadership. *Whilst this pathway is being delivered virtually, it is not a requirement for participants to have completed the Leadership Pathway as a pre-requisite, although it is recommended.*
Delivery	**National Delivery using a virtual platform.**
Outcomes	<ul><li>Connect the Church's mission and theological foundations with the concept of "healthy cultures" and safeguarding principles, so that "safeguarding" is embedded in their beliefs and values, not just intellectually.</li><li>Analyse leadership behaviours that are needed to promote healthier cultures (including how to involve and empower others) and feel confident and determined to demonstrate them.</li><li>Reflect on the kind of healthy culture that is protective, preventative, healing, and restorative.</li><li>Strengthen team working, sharing, supporting and role modelling in respect of safeguarding.</li><li>Show strengthened values and beliefs in respect of safeguarding by reflecting on their own leadership style and how their own personal life journeys and backgrounds can impact on their intellectual, emotional, and practical responses to safeguarding.</li><li>Develop a deeper intellectual and emotional understanding of the nature of harm and abuse and its impact on victims and others (both individuals and communities /organisations) in the Church.</li><li>Translate the above learning outcomes into new and observable leadership behaviours which deliver measurable safeguarding outcomes and demonstrate that safeguarding is at the heart of everything they do.</li></ul>
Required Attendees	This pathway is for members of the senior leadership team of a Church body who have, in different ways, responsibility for, and involvement in, safeguarding matters:<ul><li>Archbishops</li><li>Diocesan and Suffragan Bishops</li><li>Provincial Episcopal Visitors</li><li>Archdeacons, including Associate Archdeacons</li><li>Deans</li><li>Executive Chapter Members/Residentiary Canons (non-executive Chapter members are trained at Leadership level unless their role in the diocese requires a higher level)</li></ul>

	• Bishops' Chaplains
	• Diocesan Secretaries/Chief of Staff/Chief Executive/Cathedral Administrators
	• Directors of Communications
	• Directors of Ministry
	• Registrars
	• Diocesan and Cathedral Safeguarding Officers
	• Directors of Music/Masters of Choristers
	• HR Directors
	• Senior Chaplains to the Armed Forces
	• TEI Principals
	• Leaders of Religious Communities
Recommended Attendees	Not Applicable

Fidelity to the Pathway	Online/Virtual Delivery (May 2021 – December 2022)	In-person Delivery
	Virtual Delivery:	**This will be developed – in conjunction with survivors – after all relevant people have completed the virtual version.**
	• Three sessions delivered via Zoom (Session One is three hours, Sessions Two and Three are 90-minutes each).	
	• Each session is spaced four – five weeks apart.	
	• Two facilitators.	
	• Optimum number of participants: 12.	
	• Pre-work completed and submitted before Session One.	
	• Session One – the three questions are discussed as per the pathway.	
	• Session Two – Biblical reflection is completed. Survivor experience/perspective.	
	• Session Three – Case study exercise.	
	• Post course evaluation – Four – five weeks after Session Three is completed as set out in the pathway.	

Evaluation	Level 4 – Immediate feedback captured at the end of the learning pathway. Reflective evaluation tasks. Setting of safeguarding goals which can be discussed and reviewed by the DSA/CSA and during the person's developmental meetings over the next few years before their refresher is due and/or 360-degree feedback.

4 Additional Safeguarding Learning Pathways

4.1 Role Specific Pathways

Permission to Officiate	
Aim	To explore and reflect on the safeguarding dimensions involved in the ministry of these roles.
Pre-Requisites	Basic Awareness and Foundation
Delivery	**Local delivery using a virtual platform or in-person learning sessions.**
Outcomes	• Connect the Church's mission and theological foundations with what good leadership behaviour looks like in a safeguarding context. • Evaluate aspects of their own practice and identify changes required which they then take forward with confidence. • Analyse what healthy Christian communities look like, how healthy communities keep people safe, and their role as leaders in shaping Christian communities that are healthy and safe. • Integrate their own faith, beliefs, and values with those underpinning good safeguarding behaviours.
Required Attendees	Anyone holding PtO or who is a Reader Emeritus whose role does not meet the Leadership Pathway criterion. Where individuals hold more than one role, or serve more than one Church body, they should train at the highest required level
Recommended Attendees	Not Applicable

Fidelity to the Pathway	Online/Virtual Delivery	In-person Delivery

	• One three-hour session split into three 50-minute sections with breaks in between.
	• Optimum number of participants: 12.
	• Pre-reading materials sent two weeks prior to the session.
	• Session split into three sections –
	  ○ Section 1 – the three questions are discussed as per the pathway.
	  ○ Section 2 – Biblical reflection is completed.
	  ○ Section 3 – case scenarios exercise – choice of how many scenarios to use, and whether to retain those supplied or use another/s.
	• Post course evaluation – four weeks after session is completed as set out in the pathway.
		• One three-hour session split into three 50-minute sections with breaks in between.
		• Optimum number of participants: 24
		• Pre-reading materials sent two weeks prior to the session.
		• Session split into three sections –
		  ○ Section 1 – the three questions are discussed as per the pathway.
		  ○ Section 2 – Biblical reflection is completed.
		  ○ Section 3 – case scenarios exercise – choice of how many scenarios to use, and whether to retain those supplied or use another/s.
		• Post course evaluation – four weeks after session is completed as set out in the pathway.

Evaluation	Level 3 – Immediate feedback captured at the end of the learning pathway, reflective evaluation tasks.

	Parish Safeguarding Officer Induction
Aim	To equip learners with an understanding of the role of the Parish Safeguarding Officer and induct them into key working practices and relationships.
Pre-Requisites	Basic Awareness and Foundation
Delivery	**Local delivery using a virtual platform or in-person learning sessions.**
Outcomes	<ul><li>Understand the role, responsibilities and working relationships of the PSO, including the Local Authority.</li><li>Identify a variety of approaches to raising awareness and improving safeguarding practice.</li><li>Evaluate safeguarding information reported by members of the church or community and determining an appropriate response.</li><li>Create a development plan for local ministry to support development of safeguarding practice in their context.</li></ul>
Required Attendees	<ul><li>Persons taking on the role of Parish Safeguarding Officer</li></ul>
Recommended Attendees	<ul><li>Existing Parish Safeguarding Officers</li></ul>

Fidelity to the Pathway	Online/Virtual Delivery	In-person Delivery
	This is an induction session. It introduces participants to the role and the safeguarding team, rather than being a learning pathway. Everyone who attends this course must have completed the Basic and Foundation Pathways. <ul><li>One three-hour session.</li><li>Pre-reading materials sent two weeks prior to the session.</li><li>Optimum number of participants: 12.</li><li>Post course evaluation – four weeks after the session, completed as set out in the induction materials.</li></ul>	This is an induction session. It introduces participants to the role and the safeguarding team, rather than a learning pathway. Everyone who attends this course must have completed the Basic and Foundation Pathways. <ul><li>One three-hour session.</li><li>Pre-reading materials sent two weeks prior to the session.</li><li>Optimum number of participants: 24.</li><li>Post course evaluation – four weeks after the session, completed as set out in the induction materials.</li></ul>

Evaluation	Level 3 – Immediate feedback captured at the end of the learning pathway, reflective and practical evaluation tasks.

Link Person	
Aim	To equip learners with an understanding of the role of the Link Person and induct them into key working practices and relationships.
Pre-Requisites	Basic Awareness and Foundation
Delivery	**National delivery via Zoom**
Outcomes	● Understand the role, responsibilities, and key working relationships of the Link Person. ● Explore the case/allegations management process, including partnership working with the Diocesan Safeguarding Officer. ● Identify good practice in working with and effectively supporting respondents throughout the allegation management process. ● Reflect on the importance of self-care, supervision and pastoral support whilst performing the role of Link Person.
Required Attendees	Anyone undertaking the role of Link Person.
Recommended Attendees	Not Applicable

Fidelity to the Pathway	Online/Virtual Delivery	In-person Delivery
	Virtual Delivery: ● Three x 90-minute sessions delivered via Zoom; each session is one week apart. ● Two facilitators – delivered by the NST. ● Optimum of 12 participants ● Pre-work for Session One completed and submitted before Session One. ● Session One – facilitated discussion based upon the pre-work. ● Pre-work for Session Two – theological reflection. ● Session 2 – interactive session. ● Pre-work for Session Three – case study. ● Session 3 – interactive session ● Post course evaluation – three months after Session Three is completed as set out in the pathway, including 360 feedback and a reflective exercise.	Not applicable
Evaluation	Level 3 – Immediate feedback captured at the end of the learning pathway, reflective evaluation tasks and 360-degree feedback.	

Aim	To equip learners with an understanding of the role of the Support Person and induct them into key working practices and relationships.
Pre-Requisites	Basic Awareness and Foundation
Delivery	**National delivery via Zoom**
Outcomes	• Understand the role, responsibilities, and key working relationships of the Support Person. • Explore the skills and knowledge needed to undertake effective pastoral care, including a particular focus on trauma informed approaches. • Identify appropriate ways to support survivors, both during and after a disclosure has been made, and throughout the allegation management process. • Reflect on the importance of self-care, supervision and pastoral support whilst performing the role of Support Person.
Required Attendees	Persons taking on the role of Support Person
Recommended Attendees	Not Applicable

Fidelity to the Pathway	**Online/Virtual Delivery**	**In-person Delivery**
	Virtual Delivery: • Three 90-minute sessions delivered via Zoom; each session is one week apart. • Two facilitators – delivered by the NST. • Optimum number of participants: 12. • Pre-work for Session One completed and submitted before Session One. • Session One – facilitated discussion based upon the pre-work. • Pre-work for Session Two – theological reflection. • Session Two – interactive session. • Pre-work for Session Three – case study. • Session 3 – interactive session. • Post course evaluation – three months after Session Three is completed as set out in the pathway.	Not applicable

Evaluation	Level 3 – Immediate feedback captured at the end of the learning pathway, reflective evaluation tasks and 360-degree feedback.

	Diocesan Directors of Ordinands/Assistant Diocesan Directors of Ordinands
Aim	To equip the learner with an understanding of the significance of their role in ensuring safeguarding is a central feature of formation.
Pre-Requisites	Basic Awareness, Foundation and Leadership
Delivery	**National delivery via Zoom**
Outcomes	<ul><li>Connect the Church's mission and theological foundations with the need to be rigorous about examining candidates in respect of safeguarding.</li><li>Understanding the theological imperative of safeguarding, and the true nature of forgiveness, reconciliation, and redemption.</li><li>Recognise and be prepared to respond to candidates who have their own experiences of abuse. Explore issues of power and authority and how individuals and institutions can be groomed and how confidentiality can be used to create confusion around safeguarding.</li><li>Show strengthened values and beliefs in respect of safeguarding by reflecting on their own unconscious biases and how their own personal life journeys and backgrounds can impact on their intellectual, emotional, and practical responses to safeguarding individuals and communities /organisations in the Church.</li><li>Translate the above into transparent decision making and record keeping.</li></ul>
Required Attendees	Diocesan Directors of Ordinands and Assistant Diocesan Directors of Ordinands.
Recommended Attendees	<ul><li>Bishops Advisory Panel Advisers</li></ul> *Others may be added later – subject to ongoing development discussions with the National Ministry Team*

Fidelity to the Pathway	Online/Virtual Delivery	In-person Delivery
	Virtual Delivery:<ul><li>Three 90-minute sessions delivered via Zoom; each session is one week apart.</li><li>Two facilitators – delivered by the NST.</li><li>Optimum number of participants: 12.</li><li>Pre-work for Session One completed and submitted before Session One.</li><li>Session One – facilitated discussion based upon the pre-work.</li><li>Pre-work for Session Two – theological reflection.</li><li>Session 2 – interactive session.</li><li>Pre-work for Session Three 3 – case study.</li><li>Session 3 – interactive session.</li><li>Post course evaluation – three months after Session Three is completed as set out in the pathway.</li></ul>	Not Applicable
Evaluation	Level 3 – Immediate feedback captured at the end of the learning pathway, reflective evaluation tasks and 360-degree feedback.	

4.2   Issue Based Pathway

Raising Awareness of Domestic Abuse	
Aim	To equip participants to engage thoughtfully and proactively with the issue of domestic abuse and those affected.
Pre-Requisites	Basic Awareness and Foundation
Delivery	**Online Delivery** (*Replica of online material available for in-person delivery in exceptional circumstances*)
Outcomes	• Identify the typologies of domestic abuse and survivor groups. • Explore myths, barriers, stereotypes and impacts of domestic abuse particularly in a faith context. • Reflect on how your own beliefs and values and the stories and narratives that they bring impact on your responses to survivors and perpetrators. • Evaluate the needs of domestic abuse survivors to support them effectively, including referral pathways and the roles of supporting agencies. • Identify safeguarding actions to protect victims or those at risk whilst also understanding the limitations and boundaries of your role.
Required Attendees	**Raising Awareness and In-Person Extension** • Anyone holding the Bishop's licence, commission, authorisation, or permission (clergy, PtO, Readers, LLMs) • Bishops' Visitors/Pastoral Visitors • Safeguarding Officers • Ordinands during IME 1. • PCC Members/Lay Chapter Members. • Staff at Theological Education Institutions with student facing roles. • Members of the Diocesan Safeguarding Advisory Panel.
Recommended Attendees	• Persons holding any other pastoral role within the Church
Fidelity to the Pathway	**Online/Virtual Delivery** / **In-person Delivery** Raising Awareness – Completed online. • In-person delivery in a single session by exception using the material provided by the NST. • Optimum number of participants: 24.
Evaluation	Level 2 – Immediate feedback captured at the end of the learning pathway and reflective evaluation tasks.

4.3   Toolkits

	Safer Recruitment and People Management
Aim	To equip participants with an understanding of safer recruitment, and the skills and practices necessary to promote positive safeguarding behaviour (and detect safeguarding risk) once a person is in role.
Pre-Requisites	Basic Awareness and Foundation
Delivery	**Online Pathway** (*Replica of online material available for in-person delivery in exceptional circumstances*)
Outcomes	• Reflect theologically on personnel recruitment and safer people management. • Understand the recruitment and people management process, its intersection with relevant legislation, and how each stage contributes to safer people management. • Explore good people management practice to be implemented once a person is in post/role. • Create a contextually relevant personal management plan that reduces risks.
Required Attendees	• Line managers and anyone involved in the recruitment of Church Officers (employees, elected members, and volunteers). • Those with responsibility for administering DBS. • Safeguarding Officers in all Church bodies. • Ordinands during IME 1.
Recommended Attendees	Not Applicable

Fidelity to the Pathway	**Online/Virtual Delivery**	**In-person Delivery**
	Completed online.	• In-person delivery in a single session by exception using the material provided by the NST. • Optimum number of participants: 24.

Evaluation	Level 2 – Immediate feedback captured at the end of the learning pathway and reflective evaluation tasks.

5 Professional Development for Safeguarding Staff

DSA/CSA Development

One of the structural vulnerabilities of the Church's current safeguarding arrangements is that there is no formal induction and professional development programme for Diocesan and Cathedral Safeguarding Advisers.

DSAs/CSAs come from a variety of professional backgrounds and to a large extent must find their own way in developing their DSA/CSA role. This will inevitably mean variation in how the role is interpreted and does not allow for DSAs/CSAs to continuously develop their skills and knowledge in the unique circumstances of the Church context.

A professional development programme for DSAs/CSAs will comprise delivery of an initial ten days over 18 months (2021/22), followed by two days for each subsequent year.

It is anticipated that by the time the elements of the programme are identified and commissioned it will be possible to deliver these in-person.

The development of this programme will now also consider the development of the Diocesan Safeguarding Adviser role as set out in the IICSA recommendations which have been accepted by the House of Bishops.

The programme will include:

- Risk Assessment

Trainers Development

A five-day professional development programme over a 12-month period (2021/22) for safeguarding trainers[12]. This will be followed by an additional two days of development each year.

This is imperative as the new learning and development framework is based on a blended learning approach requiring those who deliver the pathways to be skilled in a range of methodologies.

The programme content will be designed alongside Safeguarding Trainers.

---

[12]   This applies to safeguarding trainers employed by Church bodies and not to volunteer trainers.

6　Additional Development Opportunities

In addition to the safeguarding learning pathways detailed above, additional development opportunities will be offered by the NST. These additional opportunities will be arranged/commissioned/delivered nationally in response to safeguarding developments for a range of attendees across Church bodies.

Examples of such opportunities will include:

- Workshops for each diocese and cathedral (combined) to explore issues of healthy culture, including spiritual abuse. These workshops will be offered as an option and do not have to be accepted by each area.

- Workshops to share the content of the Senior Leadership Pathway with those not participating but with an interest (i.e., Chairs of Diocesan Safeguarding Advisory Panels).

- Networking days for DSAs/CSAs/Safeguarding Trainers (including trainers within TEIs)/DSAP Chairs (at least annually).

6.1　MSc Leading Safer Organisations: Safeguarding for Senior Leaders

For several years development has been underway, in partnership with the University of Lincoln, of a post-graduate level qualification in safeguarding and senior leadership. Initially the idea of two of our Diocesan Safeguarding Advisers, the NST has been involved in the development and discussions around this programme for some time. We are now in the exciting position of seeing this programme come to fruition. Over the next 12 months there will be more information to share in respect of the project but for now, the overview is as follows:

The MSc Leading Safer Organisations: Safeguarding for Senior Leaders is a part time, modular programme, composed of 180 credit points at level 7 (M level). The title reflects the emphasis of the degree; it is not primarily for professional safeguarding officers within organisations, but for senior leaders who have the overall responsibility for creating and leading cultures that are protective rather than harmful, but who do not have a professional background in safeguarding. The degree is aimed at senior leaders from several sectors including faith, sport, the arts, charities, non-government organisations (NGO) and across the voluntary sector.

The quality of leadership and practice within institutions is critical in protecting children and adults at risk of harm, and in preventing and responding to abuse. Leaders have a key role and responsibility in improving culture and practice in responding to vulnerable children and adults. Leaders need to model the right behaviours and values, including engaging in open and honest dialogue within their organisations to promote and ensure safe practices. The programme aims to be reflective of cutting-edge thinking, practice, and research in safeguarding and in leadership, drawing on contemporary issues nationally and internationally. To support the programme national and international leading academics, practitioners and organisational leaders will be invited to contribute to the design, development, teaching, learning and assessment of the programme.

7 Quality Assurance

The Church has committed to developing a set of National Safeguarding Standards as part of a quality assurance framework. The quality assurance framework under development will be a mechanism for:

- Asking and answering the question: "How well are we doing this and what is the difference/outcome being achieved?"

- Analysing the answers to this question to gain learning and deepen organisational safeguarding understanding and expertise.

- Using that learned expertise to drive systematic change and continuous improvement in both the quality and impact of the activity, and to increase our knowledge and understanding of the evolving nature of church-based abuse.

Under the new quality assurance framework, statements to ascertain "What good looks like" will be developed for each of the standards. One of the Standard areas to be developed is "Safeguarding expertise, supervision and support, management structures and governance". Safeguarding Learning will be part of this area, and the Standard will focus on "Safeguarding learning can be evidenced to be transformative: it results in positive safeguarding behaviours by engaging people at the level of their beliefs, values and theology."

Set out below are the "What good looks like" statements in respect of safeguarding learning which have been developed so far, and will be further developed as work on the introduction of the quality assurance framework is taken forward as part of the IICSA Recommendation 1 and 8 projects.

1   The safeguarding learning delivered is characterised by the following:

- Based on a clear theoretical model of how people learn.

- The design and methodologies used enable engagement at the level of people's beliefs and values.

- The voice and experience of victims and survivors is a key active ingredient of all safeguarding learning.

- Theological principles are linked with safeguarding imperatives and values.

- Opportunity for dialogue and self-reflexivity.

- Developing a healthy Christian culture in Church bodies, and the relationship between culture and safeguarding, are golden threads.

2   All Church bodies (parishes/dioceses/cathedrals/TEIs/religious communities) can evidence whether their safeguarding learning is impacting on participants' behaviours.

3   Participants of the Leadership/Senior Leadership Pathways can evidence changed behaviours in respect of safeguarding as a result of their completion of the Pathway.

4   Participants of the Leadership/Senior Leadership Pathways will not be deemed to have successfully completed the Pathway until they have completed all elements including the evaluation stage.

5   Safeguarding learning is co-led by facilitators who together can bring the required level of safeguarding and learning delivery/facilitation expertise.

6   Church bodies have in place a strategy for the involvement of survivors in learning pathways and can demonstrate how they have involved survivors in-person in the delivery of learning pathways.[13]

7   Church officers are up to date with their safeguarding learning requirements.

8   An adequate level of resource is secured to enable the required level of learning to be delivered.[14]

Supervision and on-going development of safeguarding trainers

9   The national Church has in place a continuous professional development programme for those who deliver safeguarding learning pathways.

10   Safeguarding trainers can evidence the positive impact of their learning from the development programme on their own practice.

11   Those who deliver safeguarding training are observed – at least annually – to demonstrate an understanding of, and ability to deliver effectively, a range of learning methodologies.

---

[13]   The NST will support Church bodies in achieving this where possible and when appropriate. This is not always achievable, and not always suitable. What is critical is to incorporate survivor voice.

[14]   It is recognised by the NST/National Safeguarding Steering Group (NSSG) that that Diocesan Boards of Finance cannot always 'just add' suitable resource quickly and there will be Safeguarding related demands beyond training that will also need to be resourced.